AF469255

THE STEAM RAILWAY SERIES VOLUME 8

’Twixt Hatton & Harbury

Colin Walker

OXFORD ILLUSTRATORS LIMITED

First Published 1973

Printing: B.H. Blackwell Printing Department Oxford
Film: Oxford Litho Plates

ISBN 0 902280 10 4

Publishers: Oxford Illustrated Press, Shelley Close,
Kiln Lane, Oxford.

The generous facilities and assistance afforded by the Western & London Midland Regions of British Railways are gratefully acknowledged.

'TWIXT HATTON & HARBURY'

To describe Leamington as a railway centre might surprise many of the native townsfolk born and reared among the elegance of its Regency terraces and streets but a railway centre it certainly once was. There was sufficient traffic from both the Great Western and London and North Western lines, for instance, to require an engine shed in the vicinity for each company and the railway was quite a conspicuous feature in the town. The lines of the two companies came together at Leamington and were carried over the busy shopping thoroughfare of Bath Street on two girder bridges before continuing on closely adjacent viaducts for half a mile where they parted.

Of the two companies the Great Western was the dominant party. Its station served the main line from Paddington to Birmingham and Birkenhead as well as the line to Stratford on Avon, via Hatton Junction, whereas the neighbouring London and North Western building was but a branch line station catering for local trains from Coventry, Rugby and, at one time, Northampton. This book concentrates on the former Great Western side of things because of its obvious 'glamour' and also because, apart from the diesel service that ran from Nuneaton and Coventry, and the odd freight train, the former L & NWR lines offered little activity when these photographs were taken.

The title originally intended for this book, *Calling at Leamington*, had to be amended when the realisation dawned that several of the trains depicted in it had, in fact, run through the town non-stop. Without wishing to cast any slur on the Royal Spa I should imagine that they were usually pleased to do so since Leamington was not exactly situated in the best of spots geographically, particularly where down-trains were concerned. The town and its adjoining neighbour, Warwick, lies well down in the Leam and Avon valleys out of which trains had to climb. Those making for Birmingham, of course, had much the worst of it and encountered the heaviest gradients so far on the journey from Paddington when they hit Hatton bank where the line rose from the Avon vale onto the ridge of Arden sandstone north west of Warwick.

With its stretches of 1 in 95, 108, 103 and 110 over some three miles, Hatton was an interesting bank. Besides its sheer physical presence it also marked a definite psychological stage for many expresses. It represented the last real effort before Birmingham and once over the top they were as good as there. Most crews and their engines took the bank in their stride with unruffled efficiency but there were also those who allowed the climb to generate an over-anxiety or, more often, who saw it as a respite from their labours with the shovel and were determined to spend the last twenty miles or so into Birmingham in a state of decided relaxation. In either case they would build up a heavy fire for the climb and the Great Western image for blazing a smokeless trail could become distinctly 'sooted' – a mixed blessing according to whether one was travelling in the train or waiting with a camera!

The provision of a banking engine at Warwick was proof that Hatton bank was not taken lightly. The regular expresses usually ignored the engine's presence beside the station but a great many freight trains and some of the holiday extras were glad to avail themselves of its services. Not a few shy-steaming or overloaded engines have been glad to take a breather and recover their wind up the bank while the Prairie tank up front or in the rear took on most of the work up those taxing three miles! Certainly there was no shirking some hard work on Hatton and if the visuals did occasionally disappoint the audibles invariably compensated, as so many enthusiasts discovered.

The Southern climb from Leamington to the blue lias ridge at Harbury involved a longer but steadier effort up easier gradients – the steepest being a 2½ mile stretch at 1 in 187 past the remote signal box and loop lines at Fosse Road.

Both climbs ran from embankment into cutting and made a fine, curved approach to their respective summits – an approach marked in both cases by a lofty three-arched overbridge. That at the top of Hatton, which was built on the skew, afforded a popular viewing gallery for many generations of enthusiasts and also became an essential visual feature, or 'break', in the work of numerous photographers.

Harbury's overbridge was even more graceful than Hatton's and spanned the deep fossil-rich, blue lias cutting which led to a short tunnel, built very much in the Brunel style.

On high days and holidays the Birmingham-Paddington main line became a floodgate for the teeming population of the West Midlands and the banks would resound to the exhaust of hard pressed and sometimes unlikely engines coping with varying degrees of success with ten-, eleven- and even twelve-coach trains. They provided an entertaining and exciting procession but for me the principal attraction of the line was always the 'King' and 'Castle' hauled expresses which perhaps accounts for their profusion in this book. Their proud ascents to Hatton or Harbury, whether witnessed from the footplate or the lineside, remain indelible memories.

Colin Walker, 1972

1 Passengers waiting for a local service to Birmingham have their station seat conversation interrupted by No 6017 'King Edward IV' which is blasting through Hatton station after climbing the bank with the 2.10pm express from Paddington to Birkenhead.

2 The down 'Inter City' headed by No 6015 'King Richard III' carries the summit with confidence.

3 In the up direction No. 6005 'King George II' gathers speed after reaching the top of the bank.

4 An ailing 'Castle' No 5046 'Earl Cawdor' which has been losing time with a Summer Saturday express from Bournemouth is given the assistance of Banbury's station pilot No 6911 'Holker Hall'. The two are seen making a combined effort under grey skies near Hatton top.

5 From the up side No 7036 'Taunton Castle' climbs with determination below the overbridge with a football special for the West Midlands.

M16

6 Superior progress by No 6011 'King James 1' caught swinging below the overbridge with the 1.10pm Paddington-Birmingham express.

7 On a fine Summer day a beautifully-turned-out 'Castle', No. 5038 'Morlais Castle', nears the summit with the 8.35am from Bournemouth to Wolverhampton.

3856

8 Freight trains. A 2-8-0, No 3856, with a train of iron-ore hoppers.

9 On the down slow line Prairie tank No 4110 brings up a mixed freight.

10 Hatton Banker. No 5101 provides rear end assistance to an iron ore train.

11 Coupled ahead. No 5101 aids No 5011 'Tintagel Castle' which has been in difficulties for steam with the 9.15am from Margate to Wolverhampton and has stopped at Warwick to take on the banker. They are here about a mile from the summit.

5082

12 Climbing 'Castles'. A picture which suggests that Great Western engines did sometimes make smoke. The fireman of No 5082 'Swordfish' on the 9.30am Bournemouth-Birkenhead through train, having built up a thick fire, takes life easily as he hangs out from his engine, indifferent, it seems to the 'cloud' he has created above him. On the slow line a L.M. Region 8F attempts to compete.

13 No 7014 'Caerhays Castle' storms the climb with a Cup Tie special.

14 The distinctive front end of No 6000 'King George V' never failed to quicken the pulse whenever it appeared. It is here sweeping around the curve towards the overbridge in flamboyant fashion with another football special. Rattling down the grade is a fitted freight with a 28xx 2-8-0 in charge.

15 Climbing near Budbrooke. No 6015 'King Richard III' with the 1.10pm from Paddington to Birkenhead.

16 Grey weather. No 7033 'Hartlebury Castle' heads a special past Budbrooke.

17 A slow line haul by No 5983 'Henley Hall' at grips not only with the gradient but also a bitter cross wind.

18 The tower of St. Mary's Warwick, dominates the skyline on a radiant summer afternoon as 'Castle' No 5076 'Gladiator' makes handsome progress past Budbrooke signal box with the Margate-Wolverhampton express.

19 No 5093 'Upton Castle' coasts down the bank towards Warwick with the 3.35 pm from Wolverhampton to Paddington.

20 Freight trains. 8F, No 48559, fresh from overhaul, climbs out of the Avon valley with a long train of empties.

21 2-8-0, No 3817 pulls out of Warwick with a down ironstone train.

LEAMINGTON

22 A stirring departure by No 6019 'King Henry V' with the 9.10am Paddington-Birkenhead express.

23 No 6011 'King James I' passes Leamington North signal box with the 1.10pm from Paddington to Birkenhead.

M16

24 No 7029 'Clun Castle' hurries past the same signal box with the 'Return to Steam' special from Tyseley to Didcot in June 1972.

25 No 5081 'Lockheed Hudson' moves out with a Northbound express.

26 'King' departures. No 6018 'King Henry VI' with a Paddington-Birkenhead express.

27 No 6021 'King Richard II' gets under way with the down 'Cambrian Coast Express' and the fireman looks back to check the long train.

CAMBRIAN
COAST
EXPRESS
6021

28 A stopping train from Oxford and Banbury stands in No 2 platform with No 6864 'Dymock Grange' on the front.

29 Caught in the act. Driver Frank Burridge of Leamington opens No 6864's regulator.

30 Castles on the up. No 5061 'Earl of Birkenhead' in full glory waits to leave with the Birkenhead-Bournemouth express.

31 No 5084, 'Reading Abbey' strikes off with the 2.20pm Friday train from Wolverhampton to Paddington.

32 Titled trains. No. 6018 'King Henry VI' crosses the Leamington viaduct with the up 'Intercity'.

33 No 6026 'King John' puts a vigorous front forward as it blasts out with the up 'Cambrian'.

CAMBRIAN COAST
EXPRESS
6026

34 More 'Kings'. A fine 'arranged' effort by No 6022 'King Edward III' making an uncompromising start with the 8.50am from Birkenhead to Paddington.

35 No 6019 'King Henry V' does a spot of girder shaking as it crosses the bridge over busy Bath Street with the 8.55am from Birkenhead to Paddington.

V05

36 Still more 'Kings'. From the L.N.W. viaduct No. 6015 'King Richard III' is seen accelerating away with the 6.30am from Birkenhead to Paddington.

37 With a full head of steam No 6017 'King Edward IV' coasts round the curve with the 3.35pm express from Wolverhampton to Paddington.

38 'Halls'. No 4964 'Rodwell Hall' (a rough rider!)
accelerates over the viaduct in the rain with a semi-fast from Birmingham to Paddington via Oxford and Reading.

39 No 5988 'Bostock Hall' restarts an up coal train from Leamington after being held in the loop at the side of the station.

40 No 5025 'Chirk Castle' passes Leamington South Junction with the 11.5am from Wolverhampton to Bournemouth.

41 No 6019 'King Henry V' pulls off the viaduct with an evening express to Paddington.

42 Pressed into Class A service on a Summer Saturday, Mogul No 6366, with a train of Southern stock bound for the South coast, passes Leamington shed.

43 The fireman of a Nuneaton 8F, No 48287 which is making for Oxford with an up coal train from the L.N.W. line studies the symptoms of a temperamental injector while passing the South Junction.

44 No 5983 'Henley Hall' makes confident progress out of Leamington with the 10.10am from Birmingham to Margate on a Summer Saturday. A picture which makes an interesting comparison with the same engine's 'heavy weather' performance in illustration 17.

45 Steam Special. The Great Western Society's preserved 'Hall' No 6998 'Burton Agnes Hall' hurries over the viaduct with a train from Tyseley to Didcot.

V03

46 No 6029 'King Edward VIII' swings round the curve leading to Whitmash cutting with the 7.40am Birkenhead-Paddington express.

47 Evening arrival. No 1013 'County of Dorset' coasts into the spa town with a down Sunday Birkenhead express.

48 Whitnash cutting. No 6391 tackles the ten coach 10.35am holiday train from Birmingham to Hastings.

49 A low light shot of No 6005 'King George II' shortly after its final overhaul at Swindon, en route for Paddington through Whitnash cutting with the 8.50am from Birkenhead. ▶

V03

50 No 5076 'Gladiator' nears the end of the cutting with the Wolverhampton-Margate express.

51 Out in the open. No 4979 'Wootton Hall' makes a magnificent effort ▶ between Whitnash and Fosse Road with a Summer extra.

52 Signalman Gilkes at Fosse Road Box watches the smug progress of No 6000 'King George V' approaching his box with the Bulmer's Cider Special.

53 No 6027 'King Richard I' passes Fosse Road with the 8.50am from Birkenhead to Paddington.

V04

54 Harbury Cutting. No 5038 'Morlais Castle' coasts down from Harbury Tunnel with the 9.20am from Bournemouth West to Wolverhampton.

55 No 5033 'Broughton Castle' curves below the three arch bridge on the approach to the tunnel with the 9.30am from Birkenhead to Bournemouth

56 Harbury Tunnel. No 6008 'King James II' approaches the North portal with a Paddington express.

57 No 6012 'King Edward VI' dashes out with 7.20am express from Pwllheli to Paddington.

6012

◀ 58 No 7029 'Clun Castle' makes its exit with an up express.

59 A late-running and overloaded 'Castle' No 5088 'Llanthony Abbey' drags the up 'Cambrian Coast Express' through Harbury station.